GREATEST FOOTBALL STARS

ACCESS THE ACTION!

Scan the QR code to hear this story for

FREE!

Published in the UK by Sweet Cherry Publishing Limited, 2025
Unit 4u18, The Book Brothers Business Park, Tolwell Road,
Leicester LE4 1BR, United Kingdom

Sweet Cherry Publishing Limited
Unit 31, The Pottery, Bakers Point,
Pottery Road, Dún Laoghaire,
Dublin A96 EV18, Ireland

2 4 6 8 10 9 7 5 3

ISBN: 978-1-80263-541-6

Greatest Football Stars:
Bobby Charlton

Text by Luke Paton
Illustrations by Sophie Jones

This book is not authorised, licensed or approved by Bobby Charlton. Any faults are the publisher's, who will be happy to rectify for future printings.

www.sweetcherrypublishing.com

Printed and bound in Turkey

FSC
www.fsc.org
MIX
Paper | Supporting responsible forestry
FSC® C111584

Sweet Cherry

BOBBY CHARLTON

THE UNOFFICIAL STORY

WRITTEN BY
LUKE PATON

CONTENTS

1
MUNICH

On the 6th of February 1958, Bobby Charlton boarded British European Airways Flight 609 at Munich-Riem Airport for the third time that night.

Captain James Thain and his co-pilot had stopped the plane's first two attempts at take-off because there was a 'slight engine fault' that needed to be fixed. The Manchester United players and staff had been prepared for a long delay. Snow was continuously falling, covering the runway, and low clouds hung all around the airport. The weather was the worst Bobby had ever seen it.

Midfielder Duncan Edwards wasn't expecting to go home that night and had sent a telegram to his landlady: *All flights cancelled. Flying home tomorrow.*

But then everybody had been called back to the plane for one last try.

Third time lucky, perhaps?

Bobby walked down the aisle, found his seat and strapped himself in. For some reason, he didn't take his overcoat off – nor did he speak to his teammate, Dennis Viollet, sitting next to him. He only stared out of the window.

The players and staff got settled around him. Rather than laughing, joking and celebrating their European Cup quarter-final victory, they were all eerily quiet. The airport crew had reassured them that everything was fine now, but the

passengers weren't so sure. Bobby noticed that his teammates Kenny Morgans and David Pegg had changed seats. They said they thought they'd be safer at the back of the plane if anything happened.

'Now or never,' mumbled full-back Roger Byrne.

'If this is it, I'm ready,' said forward Billy Whelan.

Bobby tried not to think about what could go wrong. There wasn't anything he could do. He trusted that the airport crew knew what they were doing.

The engines roared to life, then the plane sped up and rushed down the runway.

Bobby watched the snowy field beyond the airport speed by his window ... but it didn't seem to be speeding by quite fast enough.

Knowing they were running out of runway and not trusting that the plane would get off the ground, Bobby instinctively lowered his head and prepared for impact.

The plane crashed through a fence at the end of the runway and

smashed into a house.

One of the wings was pulled away, some of the tail was ripped apart, the house caught on fire, a tree and a hut clattered into the cockpit ... and then there was a deafening explosion.

Bobby heard the horrific sound of metal grinding on metal.

Sparks.

Banging.

Then nothing but blackness.

Bobby was unconscious for ten minutes. When he woke up, he

heard sirens and saw the horror of the wrecked plane in front of him. He realised, slowly, that he was outside of the plane but somehow still in his seat.

Beside him, Viollet was lying on the floor. He was hurt, but thankfully he was alive.

'What's the matter, Bobby?' Viollet asked, clearly in shock. 'What's gone on?'

'Dennis, it's dreadful,' Bobby replied.

Bobby was still dazed and confused when he was taken to the local hospital.

How could I survive that? he wondered. *How could anyone survive?*

Then came the question that would haunt Bobby for the rest of his life: *Why did I survive?*

2 FOOTBALLING FAMILY

Bobby Charlton was born on the 11th of October 1937. He grew up in the coal-mining town of Ashington in Northumberland, surrounded by a football-loving family.

While he was growing up, Bobby always knew he had two options when it came to his future career.

The first option was to follow in his father's footsteps and become a coal miner, but mining was a very hard job. Whenever Bobby went to the top of the mineshaft with his father, he often saw the miners creeping out of the shafts – all covered in dirt and blinking in the sunlight. They looked exhausted. Even though Bobby's father was proud of his trade, it was not a job Bobby wanted for himself.

Bobby's second career option was much more exciting: to become a professional footballer. Most children don't grow up believing they can easily do this, but most children don't have the same family as Bobby Charlton.

Many of the men in Bobby's family were already footballers. His uncle Jack played for Leeds United and Bradford City. His uncle George played for Leeds United and Chesterfield. His uncle Jimmy played for Leeds United and Bradford Park Avenue. His uncle Stan played for Chesterfield, Leicester City and Rochdale.

And the footballing talent doesn't end there! Bobby's second cousin was Newcastle City legend Jack Milburn.

It goes without saying that football was in Bobby's blood, and he immediately stood out when he started playing for his primary school's team.

One day during school, Mr Hamilton (the headteacher) found Bobby and said, 'Charlton, Bobby Charlton, come with me.'

Young Bobby did as he was told. Mr Hamilton was not a man to be messed with. Only the other day, he'd dropped Bobby's friend from the football team for swearing in the playground. And Bobby couldn't think of anything worse than being dropped from the football team!

He followed Mr Hamilton down the corridor and tried to remember what he'd done wrong. Bobby had no idea what it could be, but he wasn't about to argue with his headteacher.

They stopped by a cabinet, where Mr Hamilton picked up a package. He unwrapped it to reveal ... a crimson football shirt.

'It's the finest shirt that's ever been made,' he said. 'It's our new strip.'

It's the most beautiful thing I've ever seen, thought Bobby.

Mr Hamilton told Bobby to put on the new shirt and run back into the classroom.

'Run into the classroom?' asked Bobby. He'd never been asked to run into a classroom by a teacher before!

'Aye, Bobby lad, run into the classroom,' said Mr Hamilton. 'You're the team captain. Go on. This is a great day.'

Bobby jogged back into the classroom

wearing the shirt. Mr Hamilton led the pupils in a brief rendition of the theme tune for *Sports Report*, a popular radio programme at the time. Everybody clapped at the end of the song.

It was the best day of Bobby's school life. Now more than ever, he was determined to become a professional footballer.

Bobby's mother, Cissie, was very proud of her son. Cissie loved football almost as much as Bobby. She coached a team for little children and would often kick a ball around with Bobby and his brother Jack. Sometimes she even let her sons play in the house, using furniture as the goal. Bobby loved diving across the floor in their makeshift matches!

But it was his grandfather, Tanner, who had the biggest influence on young Bobby. Tanner would tell him,

'If you are good enough, lad, there is nothing you can't do – not if you look after yourself, not if you give it everything you have.'

Bobby was already giving football

everything he had. He was at his happiest with a ball at his feet, and he played the game as often as he could. On Sundays, he and Jack went to the local park to find a match. Sometimes they'd be out there playing from 8 a.m. until 8 p.m.

It wasn't long before people recognised how talented Bobby was. Adults picked him to be on their football teams when he was only nine years old!

The crowning glory of Bobby's early footballing career came in a school match against St Aloysius in

Newcastle, while Bobby was playing for Bedlington Grammar School.

St Aloysius was a good side. They had many strong players and quickly took a 2-0 lead over Bedlington. But Bobby didn't like losing, and he was determined to turn the game around.

I can really influence this game, he thought. *I can shape it according to my will.*

Through sheer force of character and incredible skill, Bobby inspired his team to claw back control and score a goal! And then another!

At 2-2, he sensed his Bedlington teammates growing more and more confident. He knew they had it in them to win this thing! Bobby pushed forward.

Before the final whistle, Bobby fired home the winning goal with a stunning volley. It felt so good! His teammates hoisted him up on their shoulders and celebrated as if they'd just won the World Cup.

Tanner is right, Bobby thought. *If you try hard enough, if you really want something, you can get it.*

3

A GRAND ADVENTURE

After leaving the Bedlington Grammar School team, Bobby went to East Northumberland Boys and then to East Northumberland Juniors. It wasn't long before he was also playing for England Schoolboys, which meant Bobby got to represent his country!

By then, scouts from all the major clubs were sniffing around after Bobby. As many as *eighteen* clubs showed interest in him. Once, there were two scouts in his house at the same time trying to get him to sign for different clubs.

One scout from Wolverhampton Wanderers showed him a drawing of their new ground. 'Look, you must join us,' he said. 'You will be playing on pitches like that!'

Other offers from Arsenal and Manchester City were enough to get Bobby interested … but there was only ever one club Bobby truly wanted to play for.

Back in 1948, when Bobby was only ten years old, Manchester United played Blackpool in the FA Cup final. It was one of the best finals in history, and Bobby had listened to the match on a friend's radio. He fell in love with Manchester United (nicknamed the Red Devils) right there and then. Bobby followed the team from that point onwards.

So it was an exciting and nerve-wracking day in 1953 when someone told him, 'There's a scout from Manchester United watching you today, Bobby.'

Bobby was playing for East Northumberland Boys against Jarrow, and it was hardly the ideal match to impress a scout. It was a misty day and the pitch was frozen, so the playing conditions were almost impossible.

After the match, Bobby thought his performance was ordinary at best.

But Joe Armstrong, the scout from Manchester United, thought differently. He had to peek through the mist to see Bobby play, but he liked what he saw. He thought, *He's a gazelle and shoots as hard as any grown man, but he's a kid of only fourteen!*

The scout approached Bobby after the final whistle. He said, 'My name is Joe Armstrong and I'm from Manchester. I want to know if you would like to play for Manchester United when you leave school this summer.'

Bobby didn't know what to say. It really was like a dream come true!

He accepted the offer.

Armstrong had no trouble convincing his Manchester United bosses to sign Bobby. 'This lad is going to be a world beater,' he told them confidently.

Bobby was still only fifteen years old when he started his grand adventure at Old Trafford. He was picked up at the train station by Manchester United's assistant manager, Jimmy Murphy. Bobby asked him how far Old Trafford would be from where he was staying, and where the stadium was exactly.

'It's in Trafford Park, and you're going to love playing there,' Murphy told him.

Bobby pictured Trafford Park as a massive playground filled with green open spaces. *Thank goodness for that,* he thought. *It can't be so bad.*

In fact, Trafford Park was one of the largest industrial estates in Europe! It couldn't have been more different from the picture Bobby had in his mind.

His teammates weren't as he thought they'd be either. That first day, he met players such as Duncan

Edwards, Jackie Blanchflower and Billy Whelan. All of them welcomed him to the club with open arms.

Bobby became especially close to Alan Rhodes in those early days. This was probably because they had to share a bed in the house they stayed in while training with Manchester United!

There was only one thing Bobby didn't like about his new life in Manchester, and that was his job at an electrical firm. His mother had

wanted him to have a back-up plan just in case his trial with Manchester United didn't work out, so Bobby had promised to learn how to be an electrical engineer.

Bobby did the job as best he could and always got there on time, but his heart wasn't in it. He longed for the day when all he had to do was play football.

And thanks to all of his hard work, that day wasn't far away.

4

THE BUSBY BABES

Matt Busby was Manchester United's manager when Bobby joined the club. He had been in charge since 1945, and he was fast becoming a legend in the city.

Busby didn't see age as a barrier to the Manchester United first team.

He simply said: 'If you're good enough, you'll be able to do it.'

The 1955 team had an average age of only twenty-one, and the 1956 team had an average age of twenty-two. This was very unusual for a football club at the time, and people called Manchester United the 'Busby Babes' because the squad were so young!

Teenage Bobby saw this as a challenge. *Manchester United has a reputation for creating young players,* he thought. *I've come to the right place.*

Word got around Manchester United that Bobby was going to be a star. He was scoring goals left, right and centre for the Manchester United reserve teams. The press had even started writing about him in their match reports.

'You'll get your chance soon, Bobby,' people told him. 'Keep scoring goals and it will be only a matter of time.'

But it took a lot longer than Bobby would have liked. It seemed that every time a space in the first team opened up, someone else got the call ahead of him.

When he was at his lowest, Bobby thought, *Well, maybe you're not as good as you think you are.*

Then one Friday afternoon, Bobby was called to Busby's office. There were only two reasons why a player

got that call: to be dropped from the club or to be called into the first team. Bobby wasn't sure what was going to happen when he opened the door.

'Congratulations,' Busby said. 'You're playing in the first team tomorrow!'

They shook hands and that was it. Bobby was finally a professional footballer!

Unsurprisingly, he didn't sleep a wink that night. He thought about everything that could go right or wrong in the game the next day, and he tried to remember Busby's beliefs about what made good football.

'We're in Trafford Park, the largest industrial estate in Europe,' Busby had said. 'And the people that work there, when they finish work at the end of the week, they want to go and see something a little bit different and a little bit exciting. You have to give them their little bit of entertainment.'

On the 6th of October 1956, Manchester United played against Charlton Athletic. It was not an important game from a club perspective. But for Bobby, it was the most important match he'd ever played.

Bobby, lad, he thought, *there are no two ways around it. You are now in paradise.*

He knew this was his only chance to show the United bosses what he could do. To prove that he deserved more minutes playing for the first team, Bobby was determined to last for the entire ninety minutes *and* score a goal!

He tried to remember what Murphy had told him during training. 'When you have control of the ball and a little space, run directly at the defence,' he'd said. 'Get them onto the back foot.'

But halfway through

the first half, everything came undone. Charlton Athletic took the lead. That was not the way it was supposed to go! This was very unexpected, as Manchester United was at the top of the First Division (the same level as the Premier League today), and Charlton Athletic was at the bottom.

The team rallied after that shock to the system, and Manchester United's Johnny Berry found an equaliser. Then, in the 32nd minute, Bobby made the most of a golden opportunity.

He controlled the ball with his right foot, then turned and found himself in sight of a goal. *Don't think about it, just hit the thing,* Bobby thought. Trusting his instincts, he took the shot and … the ball slammed into the back of the net!

Goal!

Five minutes later, Bobby scored again! This time it was a volley that screamed past the keeper.

He ended his incredible first team debut with two goals in a 4-2 victory.

In the changing room after the match, the other players clapped and congratulated him. But more than anything else, Bobby felt relieved.

You've played for Manchester United, you've done what you were there to do, he thought. *You've scored goals – no one can ever take that away.*

One thing Bobby hadn't counted on was the BBC wanting to interview him after the game. He was only eighteen years old and didn't know how to talk on national radio!

Seeing that the young player was overwhelmed, Busby told him, 'Bobby, lad, these are things you will now have to do. It is what happens when you're a football star.'

But Bobby wasn't a first team regular yet. He just made sure that whenever he came into the side he made an impact. In his first season, he played seventeen times and scored twelve goals in all competitions. He even got to play in the FA Cup final at Wembley!

Manchester United won the First Division that year with ease, and

Bobby got his first championship medal. The 1956/1957 season went down in history as a high point for the Busby Babes.

But at the time, Busby himself thought there were greater things on the horizon.

During that 1956/1957 season, Manchester United became the first English side to play in the European Cup. The competition is better known today as the UEFA Champions League, and it's the jewel in the crown of any football club lucky enough to compete for it.

The Football Association had been opposed to English clubs playing in the European Cup at first, as they thought it was a distraction from the English competitions. But Busby had a vision. 'It's the future,' he said. 'This is what the public want to see.'

The club's first European Cup campaign ended with defeat in the semi-final to Real Madrid, but they got another chance to lift the trophy in the 1957/1958 season.

Manchester United was stronger than ever going into that tournament. For one thing, Bobby was a regular first team player and scored goals whenever possible. Busby believed Manchester United had what it took to become the champions of Europe.

After beating Shamrock Rovers and Dukla Prague, the Red Devils faced Red Star Belgrade in the quarter-final. Manchester United won the first leg 2-1, then Bobby scored two away goals in the second leg to secure the team's place in the semi-finals again. This time, they were determined to make it all the way to the final!

After the second leg against Red Star Belgrade, the team boarded a flight scheduled to take them home to Manchester. They had more games to win in the First Division before they could focus on the semi-finals of the European Cup.

Everything was going fine, hopes were high and the mood was light.

But before the team made it home, the plane had to stop for refuelling in Munich ...

5

THE MUNICH AIR DISASTER

British European Airways Flight 609 carried forty-four people when it attempted to take off from Munich-Riem Airport on the 6th of February 1958. After the horrendous crash, twenty-three people sadly lost their lives. The Manchester United players who died as a result of the crash were: Geoff Bent, Roger Byrne, Eddie Colman, Duncan Edwards, Mark Jones, David Pegg, Tommy Taylor and Billy Whelan. One crew member, two journalists and three Manchester United staff members were also among those who died.

Bobby was one of the lucky ones to survive, somehow coming through it with almost no injuries.

Fearing the plane would explode, goalkeeper Harry Gregg had dragged both Dennis Viollet and Bobby away from the wreckage by their waistbands. Gregg helped many other people that day, even going back into the plane to find survivors.

Manchester United's manager, Matt Busby, also survived. Bobby found him injured among the wreckage and draped his overcoat over him to keep him warm.

Bobby and the rest of the survivors were taken to the Rechts der Isar Hospital in Munich. Bobby was still dazed when he was put in the minibus. The shock finally got to him when he reached the hospital. He ranted and raved at the nurses so much that someone gave him an injection to make him sleep.

Bobby woke up hours later in a hospital bed. A German man was in the opposite bed, and he was reading a newspaper filled with reports of the Munich crash.

'I'm sorry,' the man said.

'What happened?' asked Bobby.

The German man read Bobby a list of his dead teammates.

Bobby was heartbroken. So many of his friends … gone.

How could I survive that? he thought. *How could anyone survive?*

Why did I *survive?*

He knew his mother would be worried about him, and he managed to get a message home through the British Embassy. Bobby also spoke to her when he appeared on the TV news.

'I'd like to say a few words to my mother,' he said. 'I hope she's okay and taken it well. I'm all right.'

A few days after the crash, Bobby could finally go home to England. His brother, Jack, picked him up from the docks.

When Jack asked what had happened, Bobby said, 'I'll tell you now, but never ask me again because I'll never tell you.'

Bobby was haunted by thoughts of the people he'd lost. They never left his mind for the rest of his life. And it wasn't just Bobby who felt this way.

The whole city, especially the Manchester United football club, were consumed by an overwhelming sense of grief.

What will happen next? wondered Bobby. *Is it possible to keep playing? How will we recover?*

People were very worried that Manchester United wouldn't survive the disaster. Much of their team had tragically died, and the club had been thrown into turmoil. There were rumours that the Red Devils would have to shut down.

During this difficult time, Bobby had to decide whether he wanted to carry on playing or not. He loved football and Manchester United, but what he had been through was almost too much to bear. The club told him to only come back when he was ready.

The first game Manchester United had played after the disaster was against Sheffield Wednesday.

On the day of the game, emotions ran high all around the stadium. Fans wept as a message from Matt Busby was played over the speakers. They desperately wanted the team to win in honour of the people lost in the Munich crash.

Even though Bobby didn't think he was ready to play, he still went into the changing room before kick-off.

Two survivors from the crash were there, Harry Gregg and Bill Foulkes, but a lot of the squad had been called up from the reserves. The team and staff were now almost unrecognisable.

Bobby watched the match from the stands. Even though it was hard at first, he understood that this was the only way to carry on after such a massive tragedy. For the sake of the fans, the team and the entire club,

Manchester United needed to play more football matches.

The team played fearlessly, and the final score was 3-0 to Manchester United. The fans were glad their team had won, but it was hardly appropriate to have a wild celebration.

After the game, Bobby made up his mind about something that had been bothering him.

What am I doing here? he'd thought as he watched from the stands. *There's nothing wrong with me.*

He spoke to Jimmy Murphy, who acted as

manager while Busby recovered from his injuries.

'I have to come back,' Bobby told him. Manchester United had to continue, and Bobby would help them become bigger and better than ever before.

6

REBUILDING THE RED DEVILS

Matt Busby's first reaction after the Munich tragedy was that he never wanted anything to do with football ever again. It was his wife who made him see the light.

'If these boys had their say in this, they'd want you to carry on,' she told her husband.

That was all Busby needed to hear. He took time to recover in Switzerland and returned to the Manchester United job before the 1958/1959 season began.

It was his job to rebuild the club from the ashes, which he said would take five years.

During that period, Bobby felt big changes both at Manchester United and at home.

In 1959, a year after Munich, he met a woman named Norma Ball at an ice rink. The pair dated for a while, and Bobby loved spending time with her.

She's what I want, what I need, he thought. *I feel so good around her.*

But Bobby didn't take the relationship as seriously as he should have done at first. Norma was a strong character, and she broke up with Bobby when he stopped paying her the proper amount of attention.

Bobby didn't realise quite how much Norma meant to him until after she'd split up with him. Then, when he saw her again sometime later, he was determined to do the right thing.

'You've made a pig's ear of this once, don't do it twice,' he said to himself. 'You know this is it.'

He talked Norma into giving him another chance ... and it worked!

Everybody agreed that the relationship was exactly what Bobby needed. He started taking better care of himself, of his appearance *and* of Norma!

In 1961, Bobby and Norma got

married. They had their first daughter, Suzanne, the following year. The couple soon had a second daughter, Andrea, and stayed together through thick and thin.

Manchester United was also going from strength to strength.

They managed to finish second in the First Division in Busby's first season back in charge, then they signed players who would become almost as famous and important as Bobby. That included legendary players such as

Denis Law in 1962 and George Best in 1963.

Bobby was particularly pleased with the arrival of Best.

Back in 1960, Busby had called Bobby into his office and said, 'You can use your left foot and your right. We're struggling a bit on the left side. What about playing left wing?'

Bobby didn't like the idea, but he knew he didn't have a choice. Once Busby made a decision, there was no changing his mind.

I probably won't be out here for too long, Bobby thought.

Little did Bobby know that he'd play on the left wing for almost three years. And he hated every moment of it. True, he still scored goals and he still made an impact in games. But he didn't get the ball as much as he would've liked, and he longed to play in the middle of the pitch again.

Best was the answer to his prayers. He'd been hearing about this new football genius for a year or more by then.

Before Best made the first team,

a coach told Bobby, 'We have a lad in the reserves who is very good. He'll be playing alongside you guys soon enough.'

'Well, they say that about a lot of young players – let's wait and see,' replied Bobby, doubtfully.

Best sure showed him! He was a natural left winger, and his staggering skill with the ball thrilled the United fans ... and allowed Bobby to move back inside.

Bobby, Law and Best were very different players. Bobby liked long-range shots and powerful passes. Law liked harassing defenders and setting games on fire. Best liked to go on incredible, flair-filled runs. But they all had one thing in common: they loved finding the back of the net!

The trio quickly became icons of the new Manchester United. Their combined firepower earned them the nickname of the 'Holy Trinity'. They were the terror of defences throughout most of the 1960s!

Busby's five-year plan to rebuild the Red Devils had its ups and downs throughout the seasons. It all started to come together just as he planned in 1963 – exactly five years after the Munich air disaster.

That's when Manchester United made it to the FA Cup final.

They played against Leicester City, who were the favourites to win. Manchester United had barely stayed in the First Division that year, while Leicester had finished fourth. Leicester had also beaten Manchester United twice that season already.

It looked like Leicester would score early in the final, when Manchester United gifted them three good chances to go ahead. Fortunately, Leicester were unable to convert any of them. After that brief scare, Manchester United got their act together.

In the 30th minute, Law finally opened the scoring. David Herd then doubled Manchester United's lead in the 57th minute, getting the rebound after one of Bobby's vicious shots was deflected by the goalkeeper.

Leicester clawed one goal back ten minutes from full time, and things were poised for a nervy finish. But Manchester United proved that they were more than up for the challenge, and Herd got his second goal of the match.

Manchester United held onto the lead and won the FA Cup 3-1!

The crowd sang the club's song, *When the Reds Go Marching In*, and the players celebrated on the pitch.

Bobby knew the team weren't perfect. They still had to figure out how to win the league and how to get back to playing in the European Cup. But it was a start ... Perhaps even the start of something special.

7

THE BOYS OF '66

Throughout his Manchester United career, Bobby was also a permanent fixture in the England national team. He'd made his debut on the 19th of April 1958 against Scotland and scored his first England goal!

The Scottish goalkeeper, Tommy

Younger, shook Bobby's hand after the match. 'Congratulations on your first game for your country – and your first goal,' he'd said. 'There will be many more, laddie.'

He was right.

Bobby scored two more goals in his second game for England and secured himself a place in the 1958 World Cup squad. He didn't play in that World Cup, unfortunately, but he got his chance to play on the global stage in the next competition.

In the 1962 World Cup, Bobby was a constant and brilliant presence in the heart of the England midfield. He had an especially excellent game against Argentina in the second group game.

England beat the Argentines 3-1, and Bobby scored his first goal in a World Cup! It was a moment for Bobby to remember ... but it didn't help the team make it to the final. Brazil knocked them out of the tournament in the quarter-final.

Bobby didn't let the setback stop him from scoring goals. He became

England's highest goalscorer in 1963, when he scored his thirty-first goal for the team.

By the time the 1966 World Cup rolled around, Bobby was an essential part of the team. He wasn't the captain, but fans couldn't picture a squad without Bobby at the heart of it. Everywhere they went, even when the locals didn't speak English, football fans knew the name Bobby Charlton!

So, the pressure was really on when England hosted the World Cup in 1966.

The nation expected its team to perform. They expected Bobby to score goals. And they had been promised victory by the England manager, Alf Ramsey.

'Gentlemen,' Ramsey told his players, 'we will win the World Cup. I believe it and you must believe it, and the nation must be made to believe it. You have the ability and the character to do it, and I'm telling you it will happen.'

But neither Bobby nor England got going in their first match of the tournament against Uruguay. To everybody's immense disappointment, it ended in a goalless draw.

The England players had been banned from reading the newspapers after matches. However, most of them couldn't help but read the dreadful reviews after the game. This only added to the pressure the team already felt.

Suddenly, their second match against Mexico was a must-win game. If England didn't start winning, they'd be faced with crashing out of their own World Cup!

It fell to Bobby to ignite the team with confidence again.

In the 37th minute of the Mexico game, Bobby collected the ball in his own half, put his head down and ran at the defence. He remembered Jimmy Murphy's advice: 'If there's space in front of you, Bobby, don't be afraid to run with the ball. You've got pace!'

Bobby kept running at the Mexican defenders ... and they kept retreating from him. They were on the back foot, and he was galloping towards their goal.

If he lets me go another stride here without coming to challenge me, I'm going to have a hit, Bobby thought.

The defender didn't get any closer to him, so Bobby let loose with one of his signature power shots.

Boom! The ball practically flew through the net!

Finally, England had scored their first goal in the 1966 World Cup. The competition was starting to get interesting!

Bobby's goal released the tension that had been building up in the team.

Roger Hunt added a second goal in the second half, and England were off and running. They swept past France 2-0 and topped their group, setting up a quarter-final face-off against Argentina.

The quarter-final was going to be a very different game from the group stage matches. Argentina were a strong and physical team who weren't afraid to tackle.

The England squad watched a match between Argentina and West Germany to see just how physical the Argentinian team were, but nothing could've prepared them for how brutal that quarter-final would be. There were fouls on both sides, with players getting tripped and kicked on and off the ball. It wasn't a fun game to play, and it wasn't a fun game to watch. It became a contest of willpower.

England eventually came out on top, winning 1-0. But the only feeling in the changing room after the match was relief. England's Nobby Stiles later quipped, 'Apart from the violence, I came through with no problems.'

All that remained between England and a place in the World Cup final was Portugal.

The Portuguese were the best side England had faced so far in the tournament. Their biggest star was Eusébio, a striker many people considered to be the best player in the world.

'It's your job to remove Eusébio's potential influence on the game,' Ramsey told Stiles before the match.

'For this one match or his whole career?' Stiles joked.

But the Portugal game was a serious matter, and Ramsey wanted his team at their strongest and most prepared. This was worrying for Bobby, as he'd suffered a stiff neck after the last match against Argentina. He'd been treated for the injury, but he was concerned that Ramsey wouldn't let him play in the semi-final against Portugal because of it.

'How's your neck, Bobby? Are you fit to play?' Ramsey asked.

'I can feel it slightly, Alf, but I'll be fine to play,' Bobby replied.

'All right,' Ramsey said. 'We'll keep the same side.'

Ramsey would be thankful he made that decision. Bobby had the game of his life against Portugal.

Half an hour into the match, Ray Wilson found Roger Hunt in the Portuguese penalty area. Hunt then squared the ball to Bobby, who calmly passed it into the net before Portugal's defence could leap into action. The crowd cheered, and Bobby cheered with them!

Ten minutes later, Bobby got on the end of another free-flowing move

from the English side.

Geoff Hurst passed the ball into Bobby's feet as he thundered towards the Portuguese box. Bobby blasted the ball past the keeper, and he knew at once he'd scored an incredible goal!

England was in the World Cup final, and Bobby had scored the goals that got them there!

Bobby called home the first chance he got after the game.

'Well done, Bobby, you couldn't have done better,' said his wife, Norma.

When Bobby rejoined the team in the changing room, Ramsey was giving them a team talk. 'Gentlemen, congratulations on a fine performance and on making the final,' he said. 'You have done well for yourselves, for me and, most important of all, for your country.'

Then, as if the players needed reminding, he said, 'You have a World Cup to win on Saturday.'

8

FINAL DAY

Bobby believed that Ramsey was one of the greatest managers in England. Even when others doubted his tactics, Bobby remained sure that Ramsey had the best judgment.

'He is making a team, a strong team,' Bobby said. 'He knows what he has to do to make us more effective and he has the courage to do it.'

But when he said that, Bobby didn't know what Ramsey was about to ask him to do in the World Cup final against West Germany.

'Bobby, I want you to do something for me,' Ramsey said a day before the final. 'I want you to stick on Franz Beckenbauer for every second of the match. This boy is the only German player who can beat us. He is your responsibility. If you do your job, he will not do any damage and I'm sure we will win the World Cup.'

Bobby was stunned. He thought he was going to play the same role that saw him score two goals against Portugal. But now he was on man-marking duty? It seemed ridiculous!

But what could he do? Ramsey had made his decision. After a few seconds, Bobby replied, 'Okay, Alf. I'll do that.'

As much as he hated to admit it, Bobby knew that Ramsey was right. Beckenbauer was the star of the West Germany side. If anybody was going to find a way for West Germany to win, it was going to be Beckenbauer.

What Bobby didn't know was that the West Germany manager, Helmut Schön, had told Beckenbauer that *Bobby* was the most important player in the England team! Schön had asked Beckenbauer to man-mark Bobby out of the game.

'It's very important,' Schön told Beckenbauer, 'because you're fast enough to stay with him, to control him.'

So it was Bobby's job to man-mark Beckenbauer, and it was Beckenbauer's job to man-mark Bobby. It was a battle of the midfielders!

On the day of the final, the England squad arrived at Wembley Stadium at 1.45 p.m. It was a special day for many reasons, but it took on an even bigger significance for the Charlton family. Not only was Bobby playing in his first World Cup final, but he was also playing in it with his big brother, Jack.

Jack Charlton had become a star in the Leeds United defence, and he was a rock-solid member of the England back four. Without his incredible strength, it's doubtful

England would have made it as far as they had.

Bobby and Jack saw their family before they headed to the changing room. Their parents were thrilled about the match and wished them all the best. Bobby's wife, Norma, couldn't contain her excitement either.

'You and Jack will do your best,' said Bobby's father. 'In the end, that's all you can do.'

Norma kissed Bobby on the cheek. 'I'm confident you can achieve all that is set before you,' she said.

Then they were in the changing room, going about their usual pre-match routines. Ramsey walked among the players and shook everybody's hands. 'Not one of you has been given a task beyond your ability,' he said. 'You simply have to remember all that you have achieved so far and how hard you have worked.'

The teams lined up in the tunnel and jogged out onto the pitch in front of 93,000 fans. In ninety minutes, either England or West Germany would be the world champions!

England's captain, Bobby Moore, won the coin toss and chose for West Germany to kick off.

Bobby found Beckenbauer on the pitch and locked eyes with him. Then, to his surprise, Beckenbauer became his shadow almost as soon as the game started. But the bigger surprise was when West Germany opened the scoring just eleven minutes into the match.

This is a passing inconvenience, Bobby told himself. He thought England was too good to be behind for long ... and he was right!

Seven minutes later, Bobby Moore picked out Geoff Hurst (his West Ham teammate) in the West Germany penalty area. The ball floated perfectly onto Hurst's head and ...

Goal! England was back in the game.

But the score stayed the same through to half-time and long into the second half. The crowd did their best to cheer on the team, even singing the Manchester United song, *When the Reds Go Marching In*. The England players were playing in

red shirts, after all!

In the 77th minute, Hurst got the ball in the West Germany area and blasted a shot towards goal. The ball deflected off a West Germany defender and looped up into the air. Jack Charlton and Martin Peters raced to meet the ball before it hit the ground. Peters got there first and slotted it neatly past the keeper.

It was 2-1 to England!

Bobby ran into Nobby Stiles's arms in celebration. 'Nobby, we've won!' he shouted. 'They can't beat us now!'

There were only thirteen minutes left to play.

Bobby got a chance to score four minutes from full time when Hunt squared the ball to him in front of the West Germany goal, but he struck too early and missed.

It was a chance he would regret when three minutes later – disaster! Wolfgang Weber scored an equaliser for West Germany from close range.

Bobby felt deflated. The final whistle blew moments later.

The West Germany striker Uwe Seeler trotted past Bobby as he picked up the ball. 'Bobby, that's football,' he said.

Now they had to play extra time. That meant another thirty minutes of anxious football to see who'd be crowned the winner.

Ramsey gathered the players around for a team talk. 'You've won the game once,' he told his men. 'But it has been taken away from you. Now you must go out and win it again. You have to do something that will make you proud for the rest of your lives.'

The speech touched all the players, and England was full of energy when the match kicked off again. Alan Ball forced the keeper into a save one minute after the restart, and Bobby hit the post a few moments later.

But the decisive moment came ten minutes into extra time. Hurst fired a shot at goal that clattered the crossbar and then bounced down over the line ... Or did it?

The England players celebrated

as if they had scored, but West Germany's players complained that the ball had bounced *on* the line – not *over* it.

Bobby saw that one of the officials was waving his flag. *What's he got his flag up for?* he thought. *It was a goal!*

The referee ran to his assistant to ask whether the ball had crossed the line. The assistant said it had, and the goal was given.

It was 3-2 to England!

The West Germany players were annoyed that the referee had given the goal, but there wasn't a lot they could do about it. There were no instant replays in those days and no VAR. What the match officials decided was the final word.

The England players were thrilled! The atmosphere in Wembley became like a party. 'We want four! We want four!' the crowd chanted.

West Germany threw everything they had at the English defence in a desperate attempt to score an equaliser. England either had to stay alert or finish the game off with another goal.

So when the ball fell to Bobby

Moore in the 120th minute, he made a game-changing decision. Instead of kicking it out of play, Moore looked up, saw Hurst in acres of space and clipped the ball towards him. Hurst picked it up ... and smashed the ball into the top of West Germany's net!

The game was well and truly over at 4-2 to England!

When the final whistle blew, some of England's fans invaded the pitch to celebrate with the players. The players fell to the pitch in relief or danced with emotion.

There were tears of joy and laughter.

Bobby ran as fast as he could to his brother, Jack, and gave him a big hug.

'Well, what about that, kidda?' asked Jack. 'What about that?'

'Jackie, our lives are never going to be the same,' replied Bobby.

Bobby cried as the celebrations continued and the team accepted their winners' medals from Queen Elizabeth II.

They tried to get Ramsey to join in, but he didn't want to take anything away from his men. 'This now is for you players,' he said. 'You won it.'

Beckenbauer later admitted, 'England beat us in 1966 because Bobby Charlton was just a bit better than me.'

Ramsey also agreed that Bobby was 'very much the linchpin of the 1966 team.'

Bobby scored three goals in the tournament and was undoubtably a key player in the squad.

He received recognition for this when he won European Footballer of the Year (now called the

Ballon d'Or) and Footballer of the Year in 1966. The honour was more than a boy from Northumberland could've ever dreamt of.

There was only one more thing left to do. If he was ever going to be remembered as the very best, Bobby had to win the European Cup with Manchester United.

9

CHAMPIONS OF EUROPE

On the 29th of May 1968, Manchester United met Portuguese club Benfica in the final of the European Cup at Wembley Stadium. It was two years after the 1966 World Cup and ten years after the Munich disaster.

Bobby was certain his team were

going to win it, and not just because he wanted it so badly.

After Manchester United's semi-final victory over Real Madrid, he'd fallen to the pitch and thought, *It's ours now. We are going to win the European Cup.*

Even as he travelled to Wembley to face Benfica, Bobby still thought he was right. *We've won it in Madrid. We've won it in a place which matters so much to the club and to me.*

Part of this hope may have been because Bobby and many of his teammates were coming towards the end of their careers. At the time, Bobby was thirty years old and had been playing for the Red Devils for eleven years.

This is it, he thought. *If we don't win it this time, we will never do it.*

But Bobby knew as well as anybody that nobody gave you anything for free in football.

Benfica were an excellent side. They weren't about to roll over and let Manchester United take all of the glory. Bobby had met their star striker, Eusébio, in matches before, and he

knew just how difficult he could be on a football pitch.

The Portuguese club also had their own reasons for wanting to beat Manchester United at Wembley. Two years earlier, Manchester United had demolished Benfica 1-5 in their home stadium in Portugal. So this was a chance for Benfica to get revenge.

Bobby led the team out onto the pitch. He was the captain now, and it was his responsibility to make sure each player did their job. He also got to be the first one to hear the fans roar with fearsome force as the players lined up for the national anthems. Everybody was hoping that this was the moment Manchester United honoured the men they'd lost in the Munich disaster.

The Red Devils got an early advantage in the match when Benfica defender Adolfo Calisto picked up an injury. He couldn't be substituted off the pitch because substitutions weren't allowed in football yet, so he did his best to carry on with the injury. This gave the Manchester United forward John Aston the perfect chance to run rings around him.

'Give the ball to me, and I'll give it to John,' Bobby told his team.

But despite being able to beat Calisto, Aston and the rest of the team weren't able to get anything past the Benfica defence in the first forty-five minutes. The score was stuck at a very tense 0-0.

'Keep doing what you're doing, boys,' Busby told his players in the changing room at half-time. 'Be patient. Keep passing.'

George Best put on a show, dribbling around players and flicking the ball around the pitch. Aston also got a couple of shots on goal early in the second half.

But it was Bobby who finally made the breakthrough in the 53rd minute. David Sadler crossed the ball into the box, and Bobby delightfully flicked a header past the goalkeeper.

That makes the job quite a bit easier, he thought as he celebrated the goal.

All around the stadium, the fans began to believe that Manchester United would win the cup!

They stopped cheering twenty-six minutes later, as Benfica got the chance they'd been hoping for all game. José Torres beat Bill Foulkes to the ball and headed it to midfielder Jaime Graça.

Oh no, this is my worst nightmare, thought Bobby.

Graça didn't miss the opportunity. He drew Benfica level with less than a quarter of the game to go, and the atmosphere inside Wembley suddenly grew very nervous.

Then, in the dying minutes, Benfica had a chance to finish United off. Eusébio was straight through on goal and only had the keeper to beat. It was unlikely that one of the world's greatest players would miss such a golden opportunity.

Not again, thought Bobby.

But somehow, Eusébio blasted the ball right into the grateful hands of goalkeeper Alex Stepney.

The final whistle blew moments later, with the score still level at 1-1. The Manchester United players were glad the game was going into extra time, as it gave them a chance to rethink and regroup.

The team gratefully received leg rubs and water from the physios, but

Busby told them not to lie down. 'If you lie down, boys,' he said, 'you may stiffen up, and if that happens you might not be able to start again.'

Bobby knew from his experience at the World Cup that this was true. He might be tired, but Benfica's last-ditch efforts meant that they were even more tired. Manchester United had to strike while Benfica were down!

Three minutes after the game kicked off again, Best got the ball after a long clearance from the goalkeeper. He nutmegged an oncoming defender and ran towards the goal.

Knock it in, knock it in! thought Bobby.

Best skipped around the keeper ...

and passed the ball into the open net!

Goal! Manchester United was up 2-1!

That has to be it, thought Bobby. But the team didn't stop there.

Brian Kidd added a third goal two minutes later, and the Red Devils were cruising to victory.

In the 99th minute, Kidd picked up the ball near the Benfica goal and dribbled around two defenders. He looked up and saw Bobby at the near post. He played him in.

Well, okay, thank you, thought Bobby. He gladly accepted the ball and looped it over the keeper.

Bobby's goal made the score 4-1!

'It's all over!' the commentator screamed. 'Manchester United have done it!'

Manchester United were the European Cup winners! Bobby led the team up the Wembley steps to receive the magnificent trophy.

'Well done, Bobby Charlton,'

said the commentator. 'Well done, Manchester United!'

Bobby found Busby after the game to hug him. Bobby and Foulkes were the only players still in the team who had been in that Munich crash, so it was the perfect ending for both them and their manager.

'They've done us proud,' Busby told the reporters. 'They came back with all their hearts to show everyone what Manchester United are made of. This is the most wonderful thing that has happened in my life, and I am the proudest man in England tonight.'

Since that harrowing day in Munich, Bobby had won the First Division, the FA Cup, the World Cup *and* now the European Cup. He'd achieved everything he'd ever wanted and much, much more.

Not for the first time during his career, Bobby thought, *I'm a lucky lad. A lucky lad.*

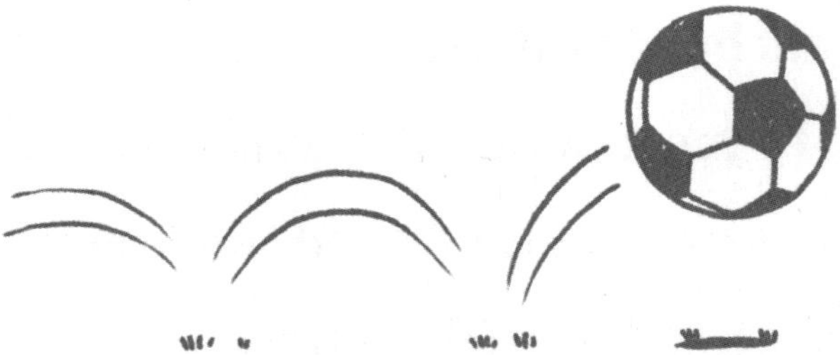

10

BOBBY'S LEGACY

Bobby played his last official game for Manchester United on the 28th of April 1973. Their opponents were Chelsea.

Thousands of people turned up to show their support and watch him play one last time. So many, in fact, that Chelsea's Stamford Bridge had to be closed an hour before kick-off because there was no more room in the stadium!

Even though Bobby didn't want to make a fuss, the teams still wanted to pay their tributes to him – an iconic player. He was made to enter the pitch on his own, while the other players formed a tunnel and applauded as he walked through it. The crowd joined in with applause, too.

There was a brief ceremony, and Bobby was given a unique award to celebrate his record-breaking time with the club.

Unfortunately for Bobby, Manchester United lost the game 1-0. 'I wanted us to play better for my last game,' he said afterwards.

The result was actually part of the reason why Bobby was retiring from football. Manchester United wasn't the same club as it had been in his prime. Matt Busby had already moved on, and Bobby was thirty-five years old. It was time for the next generation to step up.

In an ideal world, Bobby would've played football until he was seventy years old. But when he reached his mid-thirties, training and playing became less enjoyable. *I'm not sure how long I can go on,* he'd thought on some days.

Retiring still wasn't a decision he took lightly, so he asked his wife for some advice.

'Bobby, only you can really decide,' Norma told him. 'You know better than anyone else how you truly feel.'

If he was honest, he had already achieved more than anybody could dream of. When Bobby fully retired from football in 1973, he held many unbelievable records for both club and country.

He'd stopped playing for England after the 1970 World Cup, making 106 appearances for his country in total. This was a record-breaking number at the time, and only six other male players have beaten it to this day.

Bobby scored forty-nine goals for England – a record that lasted nearly fifty years until Wayne Rooney broke it in 2015.

He also made a record 758 appearances for Manchester United. This was a club record for nearly fifty years, until Ryan Giggs beat it in 2008. Bobby's 249 goals for

Manchester United was another club record he held for four decades, until Wayne Rooney overtook him again in 2017.

Although others have overtaken Bobby's records on the pitch, they'll never replace his impact off it. He was, in many ways, the perfect example of an English footballer.

In the *Daily Mirror*, Bobby Moore wrote: 'In deepest, dustiest South America, the only two words the locals ever knew in English were "Bobby Charlton". It was the same in the farthest corners of Europe.

Everywhere he went, crowds would recognise him and wave to him, and ask for his autograph ... Football will not see his like again.'

Bobby wasn't quite done with football or Manchester United after his retirement. In 1984, he became a director on the United board. He was a big supporter of famous Manchester United manager Sir Alex Ferguson, and he watched with pride as the club returned to being a global force to be reckoned with in the 1990s and 2000s.

In 1994, Bobby earned a knighthood

to add to his OBE and CBE. For the rest of his life, he was known as Sir Bobby Charlton.

On the 21st of October 2023, Sir Bobby Charlton sadly passed away, leaving behind a legacy that Manchester United will never forget.

The Holy Trinity statue featuring Bobby, George Best and Denis Law takes pride of place outside of Old Trafford. The South Stand is also now known as the Bobby Charlton Stand.

Bobby will be forever known as a gentleman who was a giant of the game.